SOLIDS, LIQUIDS AND GASES

Robert Snedden

www.heinemann.co.uk
Visit our website to find out more information about Heinemann Library books.

To order:
☎ Phone 44 (0) 1865 888066
📄 Send a fax to 44 (0) 1865 314091
💻 Visit the Heinemann Bookshop at www.heinemann.co.uk to browse our catalogue and order online.

First published in Great Britain by Heinemann Library,
Halley Court, Jordan Hill, Oxford OX2 8EJ
a division of Reed Educational and Professional Publishing Ltd.
Heinemann is a registered trademark of Reed Educational & Professional Publishing Ltd.

OXFORD MELBOURNE AUCKLAND
JOHANNESBURG BLANTYRE GABORONE
IBADAN PORTSMOUTH (NH) USA CHICAGO

Designed by Celia Floyd
Originated by Dot Gradations
Printed by Wing King Tong, Hong Kong

ISBN 0 431 12100 1 (hardback)   ISBN 0 431 12105 2 (paperback)
05 04 03 02   06 05 04 03 02
10 9 8 7 6 5 4 3 2   10 9 8 7 6 5 4 3 2 1

British Library Cataloguing in Publication Data

Snedden, Robert
  Solids, liquids and gases. - (Material world)
  1.Matter - Properties - Juvenile literature
  I.Title
  530.4

Acknowledgements
The Publishers would like to thank the following for permission to reproduce photographs: Bruce Coleman Collection: Dr Eckart Pott p11, Stephen J Krasemann p24; FLPA: M J Thomas p21b; John Cleare: p22; Network: Peter Jordan p14; Redferns: Andrew Putler p7; Science Photo Library: p19, NASA p4, Adrienne Hart-Davis p9, Tony Craddock p10, Angela Murphy p16, Simon Terrey p29; Telegraph Colour Library: Chris Simpson p13; Tony Stone Images: Greg Pease p15, Randy Wells p18, David Madison p21a, J Sneesby/B Wilkins p23

Cover photograph reproduced with permission of Tony Stone Images: Phil Degginger

Every effort has been made to contact copyright holders of any material reproduced in this book. Any omissions will be rectified in subsequent printings if notice is given to the Publisher.

Any words appearing in the text in bold, **like this**, are explained in the glossary.

Contents

What is matter?

Matter is all around us. Everything that you see, touch, feel, smell or taste is made of matter. The sun in the sky, the hair on your head, and the scent of a cake in the oven are all forms of matter. Matter is anything that takes up space – whether it be a spinning galaxy of stars or the tiny speck of an **atom**.

A space-walking astronaut may not feel the effects of gravity but he still has the same mass as he does on Earth.

Mass and gravity

One feature that all objects possess is **mass**. The mass of an object is the amount of matter it contains. Mass is not the same as weight. The weight of an object is the effect of the force of **gravity** on the object's mass. The mass always stays the same but the weight can increase or decrease depending on how strong the force of gravity is on the object.

Every object is attracted to every other object by the force of gravity. The greater the mass of an object, the greater the gravitational force it exerts. The Earth has a much greater mass than you and so your weight is actually a measurement of the Earth's gravitational force acting on your mass.

Particles of matter

All materials are made of atoms, which in turn are made of even smaller **particles**, called protons, neutrons and electrons. Scientists have worked hard to find the tiniest building blocks of matter, the particles from which all the materials we know are made. The study of the particles that make up everything is called particle physics.

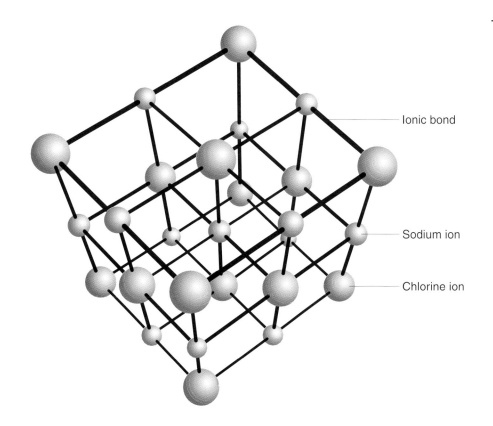

Ionic bond

Sodium ion

Chlorine ion

Atoms of different elements can link together in a variety of ways to form compounds.

Atoms, elements and molecules

Atoms can join together to form larger particles called **molecules**. Molecules are the smallest particles of an **element** or **compound** that can exist on their own without being joined to other atoms or groups of atoms. Hydrogen atoms, for example, are not found on their own. They are joined together in pairs to form hydrogen molecules. Molecules that contain atoms of one kind only are known as elements; those that contain atoms of different kinds are called compounds. Molecules vary in size from the hydrogen molecule, which is made up of two hydrogen atoms, the smallest atoms, to the complex **macromolecules** of proteins, which are essential in all living things and can contain many thousands of atoms.

Changing states

Matter usually exists in one of three forms, or states – solid, liquid or gas. The state depends on how freely the **particles** that make up the matter can move around. Most of the substances we come across will be in one of these states. Water is a good example of a substance that can be found in all three states in everyday circumstances – as solid ice in a freezer, running water from a tap and steam rising from a boiling kettle.

The changes from one state to another take place at definite temperatures called the melting point (solid to liquid) and the boiling point (liquid to gas). Changes in the opposite direction are brought about by cooling as a gas condenses to form a liquid and a liquid freezes to form a solid.

Balloon

Bicarbonate of soda

Vinegar

Try it yourself

You will need
vinegar
bicarbonate of soda
a small plastic bottle
a saucepan
a spoon
a balloon

1 Warm the vinegar in a saucepan and pour into the bottle until it is about a quarter full.
2 Put 1 spoonful of bicarbonate of soda into the balloon.
3 While holding the balloon carefully, so that the bicarbonate of soda does not fall out, stretch the neck of the balloon over the neck of the bottle.
4 Quickly lift the balloon so that the bicarbonate of soda spills into the vinegar.

The vinegar and the bicarbonate of soda will react together to produce carbon dioxide gas. As this happens the balloon starts to inflate, which shows that a gas takes up a greater volume than the same amount of a solid or a liquid.

Latent heat

A substance can be changed from one state to another by raising or lowering its temperature. The heat absorbed by a substance as it changes state (for example, from a solid to a liquid) or the heat that is released by it (from a gas to a liquid) is called the **latent heat** of the substance.

When a solid changes to a liquid, heat is taken in. When the liquid changes back to a solid, the same amount of heat is given out. This is called the latent heat of **fusion**. The amount of heat required to change a liquid into a gas is called the latent heat of **vaporization**.

Sublimation

Sublimation is an unusual change of state in which a solid changes directly into a gas without first becoming a liquid. For example, solid carbon dioxide (sometimes called dry ice) sublimes to carbon dioxide gas. When the gas is cooled it becomes a solid again.

Solid carbon dioxide, dry ice, is often used to create smoke effects on stage as it turns into a gas.

Solids

Solids are matter in a form that has a definite shape and **volume**. The volume of a material is the amount of space it takes up. The **atoms** that make up a solid are not free to move around as they are in a liquid or a gas.

Solid objects, such as stone, are rigid and hard and will keep their shape unless a physical force acts on them to change it. Some solids are **brittle** and will shatter when struck. Metals are malleable (they can be beaten into thin sheets) and ductile (they can be drawn out into wires). The properties of a solid depend on the **particles** that make up the substance and the forces acting among them. The atoms in almost all solids are arranged in regular patterns, called **crystals**.

A supercooled liquid

Glass is sometimes called a supercooled liquid. It softens easily when heated and has no definite melting point like true solids. Unlike a true solid, the particles that make up glass can move around, although very slowly. Over long periods glass can 'flow' like a liquid. The effect can be seen in very old windows where the glass is thicker at the bottom than at the top.

The atoms in a solid are not free to move but held in place by the forces that bind them together.

The particles in a solid are packed closely together and do not change position as they can in a liquid or a gas

Bonding together

The tightly packed particles that make up a solid are held together by chemical **bonds**. These are the forces of attraction that hold together atoms of one or more types of **element** to form **molecules**. The main types of bonding are **ionic** and **covalent**. The type of bond formed depends on the elements that bond together.

In ionic bonds the combining atoms gain or lose **electrons** to become **ions**. For example, in sodium chloride (common salt) a sodium atom loses an electron to form a sodium ion, while a chlorine atom gains an electron to form a chloride ion. Strong electrical forces hold the oppositely **charged** ions together. When covalent bonds are formed, the outer electrons of two atoms overlap and so are effectively shared between the two atoms.

Melting

The molecules that make up a solid are arranged so that the forces that attract and repel the molecules are evenly balanced. The molecules do not have enough energy to move to different parts of the solid but **vibrate** around these positions of balance. If the temperature of a solid is raised, the molecules begin to vibrate more strongly. Eventually the vibrations become great enough to overcome the forces that hold the molecules in place. When this happens the solid melts and becomes a liquid.

The particles that make up a solid are held together in regular patterns.

Liquids

A liquid is similar to a solid because it has a definite **volume**. However, the **molecules** that make up a liquid do not have fixed positions as they do in a solid and they are further apart than in a solid. A liquid is similar to a gas because its molecules are not fixed to each other in any particular way. The molecules in a liquid are able to move short distances but they do not have the freedom of movement found in the molecules that make up a gas.

Liquids and gases are both called **fluids** because they can flow to fit the shape of any container into which they are put. The molecules of a liquid will always follow the shape of their container, but they will not spread out in all directions to fill it.

If liquids are heated beyond a certain point, they change into gas. This is called boiling (for example, boiling water changes into steam). If liquids are cooled below a certain point, they change into solids (water freezes into ice). Different liquids have different freezing and boiling points.

Liquids take on the shape of any container into which they are poured.

Surface tension

A thin layer forms on the surface of a liquid because of the attraction between the molecules that make up the liquid. This is called **surface tension**.

Capillary action

Capillary action is the tendency of liquids to move into or out of thin tubes, called **capillaries**. It occurs whenever a liquid in a capillary is in contact with the air. Surface tension draws liquid into a capillary if the nearby capillary walls strongly attract the molecules of the liquid's surface. On the other hand, surface tension will push liquid out of a capillary if the liquid molecules are more strongly attracted to each other than to the capillary walls.

Capillary action draws water up the roots of plants. Paper towels have millions of capillaries between their fibres that absorb water by capillary action.

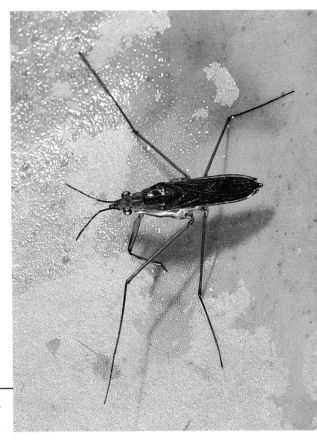

Surface tension enables a water beetle to walk across the surface of a pond without sinking.

Try it yourself

You will need
water
4 matches or wooden toothpicks
washing-up liquid
a shallow dish
a dropper

1 Put some water in a shallow dish and wait until the surface is smooth.
2 Carefully float the matches or toothpicks on the surface together so that they are all pointing inwards.
3 Using a dropper, gently put a drop of washing-up liquid in the middle of the dish between the sticks.

The surface tension in the centre is broken by the washing-up liquid and the matches immediately move out towards the rim of the dish, drawn by the surface tension on the water there.

Gases

Gas is a form of matter in which the **molecules** are free to move around randomly in otherwise empty space. A gas, such as the air that surrounds us, has neither a fixed shape nor a fixed **volume**. It will spread out to fill any size or shape of container into which it is put. All gases, whatever the molecules are that make them up, will behave in the same way.

The molecules that make up a gas are not bound together but move around randomly in all directions.

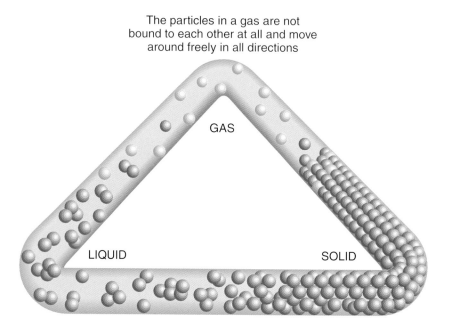

The particles in a gas are not bound to each other at all and move around freely in all directions

GAS

LIQUID

SOLID

Although you may not be able to see them, gases have weight just like solids and liquids. Because the **particles** that make up a gas are spread out thinly, a volume of gas under normal conditions will contain fewer particles and so weigh less than the same volume of a solid or liquid in which the particles are more tightly packed together.

In the air

Every cubic centimetre of air contains many billions of molecules all moving around rapidly. These gas particles are so small that they occupy only about one-thousandth of that cubic centimetre. The remaining space between the gas particles is empty. The speed at which the gas particles move is determined by their weight and by the temperature of the gas. Light particles move faster than heavy ones and the hotter the gas the faster the particles move. The gas particles are constantly colliding with each other and with the walls of any container they happen to be in. These collisions produce the effect of **pressure**.

Gases and liquids

A gas changes to a liquid when it is cooled enough for the gas particles to gather together. This is because the drop in temperature lowers the speed of the molecules and so enables attractive forces between them to bind them together. The temperature at which a gas becomes a liquid is called its **condensation point**. If the pressure of the gas is increased, it will become a liquid at a higher temperature as the particles are forced closer together allowing the attractive forces to work.

Gas laws

Gases behave according to three rules, or laws, that explain how the pressure, temperature, volume and the number of particles in a container of gas are related.

- *Boyle's law says that the pressure of a gas increases as the volume of the gas decreases. If you shrink a container full of gas the pressure of the gas in that container will increase. If you squeeze a balloon you can feel the pressure of the gas inside it resisting your squeeze.*

- *Charles's law says that a gas expands at a constant rate as its temperature rises. For example, doubling the temperature doubles the gas's volume as long as the pressure does not change. The law was developed by French scientists and hot-air ballooning enthusiasts Jacques Charles and Joseph Gay-Lussac in the 1780s. Heating air in a balloon causes its volume to increase and its density to decrease, making it lighter than the surrounding air.*

- *Avogadro's law says that equal volumes of different gases all contain the same number of particles if they all have the same pressure and temperature.*

The bubbles from this diver's breathing apparatus get bigger because the water pressure around them lessens as they rise towards the surface.

Using solids

Aircraft, like many other things around us, are made from materials called solids.

Nearly all the materials we see and use every day are solids, including the homes we live in, the furniture inside our homes, all forms of transport, from skates to supersonic aircraft, the food we eat, the books we read and the clothes we wear.

Materials scientists are more concerned with solids than with the other forms of matter (liquids and gases). We can make things with solids that are strong and will keep their shape. Although solids can become liquid if enough heat energy is applied, we tend to use solid materials that stay solid under normal conditions. Imagine your embarrassment if your clothes suddenly became liquid!

Solid to liquid and back again

Sometimes we will turn solids into liquids to make them easier to shape into the forms we need. Molten metal can be poured into moulds, for example. Once it cools and becomes solid again it can be put to use. Cement is mixed with water, sand and stones to make concrete, which dries to become a tough, strong material. Concrete has many uses, for example it is poured into place to form solid building foundations. Glass is heated and made molten to be shaped into bottles and windows.

Solid fuels

The wide variety of fuels that we use to provide us with energy come in many forms and can be either solid, liquid or gas. Coal, the most commonly used solid fuel, is used mainly to produce electricity. It is burned to create heat that is used to turn water into steam, which is then used to spin **turbines,** which generate electricity. Some coal is made into coke, an essential **raw material** in the production of iron and steel. Coal is also used to heat buildings and to provide energy for industrial machinery.

Wood has been used as a solid fuel for longer than any other material. Today, it is still an important fuel, particularly in developing countries where it is used for cooking and heating. In the industrialized nations, such as Britain, Australia and the United States, it is no longer a major source of energy.

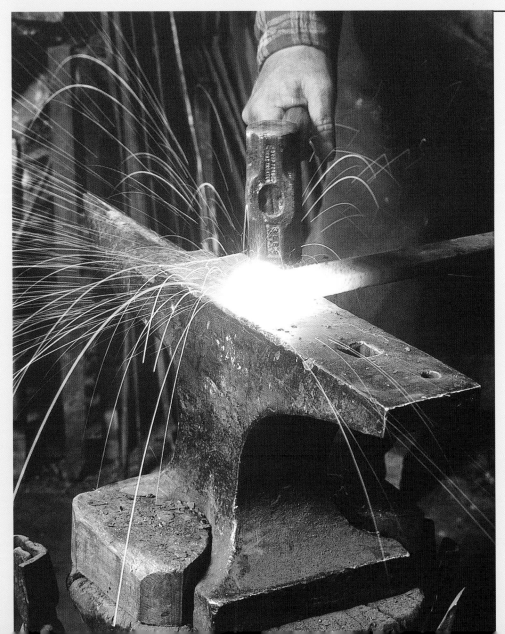

A blacksmith uses coke to produce the heat needed to soften iron so that it can be hammered into shape on the anvil.

Using liquids

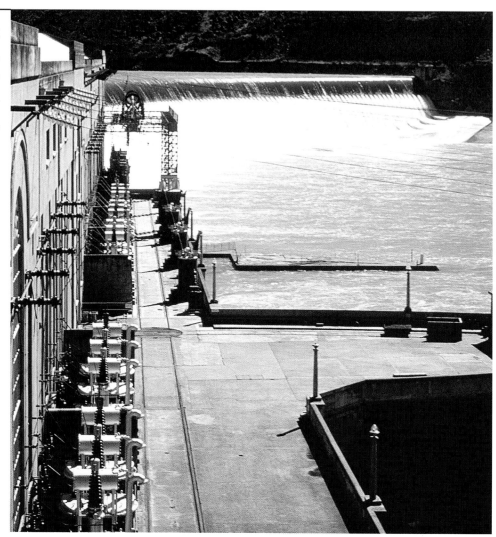

Hydraulics is the study of the behaviour of liquids at rest and in motion. **Civil engineers** use hydraulics to study the flow of water so that they can design water-supply systems for cities and towns, irrigation and sewage systems and canals. **Mechanical engineers** use hydraulics to design machines such as hydraulic **turbines**, hydraulic brakes, power-steering for cars, controls for aircraft and construction equipment.

Hydraulic machines

Water **pressure** usually supplies the power for hydraulic machines. Some hydraulic machines, such as turbines, are driven by the force of a flowing liquid. Turbines are large wheels that use the energy of the flowing liquid to power an **electricity generator**. Turbines can also be driven by gas.

Hydraulic presses increase and transfer force through a fluid from one **piston** to a larger piston and are used for lifting heavy loads and stamping out metal parts. A simple hydraulic press consists of a fluid-filled cylinder containing two pistons, one smaller than the other. A force applied to the smaller piston is transferred through the fluid to the larger piston. The force increases in direct proportion to the ratio of the area of the larger piston to the area of the smaller piston. The brakes in a car work like hydraulic presses. Pressure on the brake pedal is transmitted through a liquid to brake shoes, which press against the car's wheels.

Piston

Brake pedal

Brake fluid

Brake pad

Wheel disc

Pressing on the brake pedal transmits a force through the brake fluid to the brake pads, which press against the wheel.

Lubrication

Liquids such as oil or grease are used as **lubricants**. They are spread out in a thin film over the moving parts of a machine to prevent the parts from rubbing together and so reduce **friction**.

Liquid fuels

Liquid fuels are easy to store and transport. They are the major source of energy for cars, aircraft and other motorized vehicles, and are also used to heat buildings.

Liquid fuels are made mainly from petroleum, also called crude oil. Most petroleum is refined to produce such fuels as petrol, diesel oil and kerosene. These fuels range in appearance from clear yellow-brown oils to thick, black tars. Petrol is used to provide energy for most motor vehicles and propellor-engined aircraft. Diesel oil powers most trains, ships and large trucks, while kerosene provides the energy for jet aircraft.

17

Using gases

Some gases are lighter than the mixture of gases that make up the air we breathe, so they will rise above it. We can use this natural lifting power to get off the ground by using balloons. Hydrogen, helium and **natural gas** can all be used to inflate balloons. Hydrogen is the lightest of all gases and has the greatest lifting power but it is highly **combustible** and so not very safe. Helium is slightly heavier than hydrogen, but it does not burn and so it is much safer. Natural gas produces less lift than either hydrogen or helium but it is cheaper to produce. Gas balloons can be used for fun and for science. They have been used to carry scientific instruments 48 kilometres above the ground.

Hot air balloons make good use of the fact that increasing the temperature of a gas makes it less dense.

Gas refrigerator

The first practical refrigerator was built by Frenchman Ferdinand Carré in the 1850s. Ammonia gas dissolved in water is heated so that it boils out of the water (ammonia has a lower boiling point). The ammonia moves into a condenser where it cools and forms a liquid. It flows into an evaporator where it vaporises and becomes very cold. It then passes through the food compartment, cooling the food as it does so. The ammonia is dissolved in water again and flows back to the start of the cycle. Carré's refrigerator was too big for domestic use. Modern refrigerators use an electric motor (rather than gas pressure) to pump refrigerant gases called HCFCs.

Gas fuels

Gas fuels are an efficient way of providing energy for homes and businesses. Natural gas is used to heat buildings and cook food. It consists mainly of methane, which is colourless and odourless, so it is usually mixed with smellier compounds so that gas leaks can be detected.

Gas **turbines** are used to power **electricity generators**, ships and high-speed cars. They are also an important part of the engines in jet aircraft. Gas turbines burn fuels such as oil and natural gas and use the hot gases to spin the blades of the turbine.

Gases become liquids under pressure, which allows them to be stored in convenient containers.

Liquids from gas

Butane and propane, which make up a small proportion of natural gas, can be turned into liquids by storing them under great pressure. When the pressure is released, they change back into gas. They are easily stored and shipped as liquids. They provide a useful portable source of fuel for people on the move or who live far from natural gas pipelines.

Melting and freezing

The melting point of a substance is the temperature at which it changes from a solid to a liquid. The melting point depends partly on whether the material is a pure **element**, such as iron, a simple **compound**, such as water, or a mixture. A pure substance will melt at a definite temperature or within a narrow range of temperatures. For example, iron has a melting point of 1535°C. Increasing **pressure** lowers the melting point of a substance.

As heat is applied to a solid such as ice the temperature of the solid increases until it reaches its melting point (for ice, 0°C). At this point, even though more heat is applied, the temperature will stop rising. The additional heat increases the energy of the **molecules** in the solid, breaking the **bonds** that hold them together and causing the solid to melt. The temperature will stay at the melting point until the solid has melted entirely.

The pressure of an ice-skater's blade on the ice melts the ice, creating a thin film of water on the surface that allows the skater to glide along.

Melting mixtures

Mixtures do not melt at a specific temperature. The melting point of most simple mixtures differs from that of any of the pure substances in the mixtures. Brass, an **alloy** of copper and zinc, melts over a range of 900°C to 1000°C, although the melting point of copper is higher than this at 1083.4 °C and that of zinc is much lower at 419.58°C.

Melting points of some common materials	
Water	0°C
Iron	1535°C
Mercury	–39°C
Oxygen	–218°C

Freezing

Freezing is the change of a substance from a liquid to a solid, for example when water becomes ice. The freezing point of a substance is the temperature at which this occurs. The temperature of the substance remains at this point until all the liquid has been frozen. The freezing point of a substance is the same temperature as its melting point.

The freezing point of a liquid can usually be lowered by dissolving something in it. This is why salt is scattered on pavements during icy weather. The salt dissolves in the water, lowering the temperature at which it becomes ice – and so the ice on the pavement melts.

Gritting the roads in winter works because the freezing point of a liquid is lowered if something is dissolved in it.

Boiling and evaporation

The boiling point of a liquid is the temperature at which it changes into a gas. As the liquid is heated, the **particles** it consists of gain more energy until eventually the **bonds** holding them together are completely broken and they fly off in all directions as a gas.

Vapour pressure

The **vapour pressure** is the pressure produced by **molecules** escaping from the surface of a liquid or solid in the form of vapour. The greater a substance's vapour pressure, the faster it **evaporates**. The vapour pressure rises as the substance heats up. At the boiling point of a liquid, the vapour pressure is equal to the pressure of the atmosphere surrounding it. The lower the atmospheric pressure, the lower is the temperature needed to produce a vapour pressure equal to the atmospheric pressure, and therefore the lower the boiling point.

Melting and boiling points

Substances have different melting and boiling points because the strength of the bonds between their molecules varies. The stronger the forces of attraction between the molecules of a substance, the higher its boiling point. For example, water molecules are strongly attracted to one another and boil at 100°C. Oxygen molecules are not as strongly held together and it therefore has a much lower boiling point of -183°C. Some substances have especially strong bonds between their molecules and boil only at extremely high temperatures. Gold, for example, has a boiling point of 2807°C.

The boiling point of water at sea level is 100°C, but at 3050 metres above sea level the boiling point is about 90°C. This makes it difficult for mountaineers to make a good cup of tea!

Evaporation

Evaporation is the process in which a liquid turns to a vapour without its temperature reaching boiling point. Puddles of water left on the ground after rain eventually evaporate, and disappear into the atmosphere as water vapour. At any time, a number of the molecules in a liquid will have enough energy to escape from the forces that hold the molecules together at the liquid's surface. The rate of evaporation increases if the liquid is warmed up (for example, if the sun shines on the puddles). As the average energy of the molecules in the liquid rises, so will the number of those that have enough energy to escape.

The temperature of a liquid falls as it evaporates because the evaporating molecules remove energy from the liquid. This cooling effect is used by the body as part of its temperature control system – you cool down as sweat evaporates from your skin.

Boiling points of some common materials

Water	*100°C*
Iron	*2750°C*
Mercury	*357°C*
Oxygen	*−183°C*

These elephants are using the cooling effect of evaporation to stay comfortable.

Water

Water is the most common substance on Earth. It covers 70 per cent of the Earth's surface and is vital to the well-being of all living organisms. It is a simple chemical **compound** with remarkable properties. Its chemical formula, H_2O, tells us that each water **molecule** is made up of two **atoms** of hydrogen and one of oxygen. At everyday temperatures it can exist as a solid (ice), a liquid (water) or a gas (water vapour). Pure water is a colourless, odourless, tasteless liquid that freezes at 0°C, and boils at 100°C. Natural water in the environment is never pure because it always contains a variety of dissolved substances.

Water, water everywhere

97 per cent of the Earth's water is in the oceans and 2 per cent is in the form of snow or ice. There is less than 1 per cent available as fresh water for plants and animals.

The movement of water around the Earth is called the water cycle. Water vapour in the atmosphere **condenses** to fall as rain, flows through rivers and streams into lakes and oceans and is returned to the atmosphere as it **evaporates**.

Water as a solid (ice), liquid (water), and a gas (water vapour on the seal's breath), all at the same time!

Water and life

Water is very important to living organisms. It helps cells to keep their shape and acts as a **solvent** to dissolve salts, sugars and other substances that need to be transported around the organism; it also helps to maintain body temperature through perspiration and evaporation.

Properties of water

Water has unusual properties for a molecule of its size. The oxygen atom has a slight negative charge and attracts the slightly positively **charged** hydrogen atoms of other water molecules. The result is that **bonds** are formed between the water molecules, which holds them together. These bonds are called hydrogen bonds. This property also makes water a very good solvent for **ionic** substances, such as salts, that are formed from charged particles.

Water's unusual properties are due to the hydrogen bonds that link its molecules together.

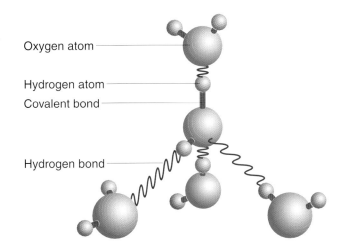

Oxygen atom

Hydrogen atom

Covalent bond

Hydrogen bond

Large amounts of heat energy are needed to produce small rises in temperature in water. A great deal of heat is required to change water from its liquid state into a vapour.

In its liquid form, water cannot be **compressed**. When it is frozen, its **volume** expands by an eleventh. Water is most **dense** at 4°C. Below this temperature, the density of water decreases because the atoms of hydrogen and oxygen in a water molecule are linked at such an angle that when water becomes a solid, the molecules join up to form a crystal-like three-dimensional pattern that is less dense than water in its liquid state. This is why ice floats on water.

Atoms in motion

Kinetic theory is an attempt to explain the physical properties of matter in terms of the movement of the **atoms** and **molecules** that make it up. **Particles** of matter are never still. No matter how solid and unmoving it might appear, the molecules of the chair in which you are sitting are constantly vibrating.

Temperature and movement

The temperature of a substance is determined by the amount of movement of the particles in it. Temperature is a measure of the average **kinetic energy** of the particles of an object. Increased temperature means increased movement. A gas is made up of rapidly moving atoms or molecules and, according to kinetic theory, it is the impact of these moving particles on a container holding the gas that accounts for the **pressure** of the gas.

Chemical kinetics

Chemical kinetics is the study of the rates of chemical reactions. For a reaction to take place, the molecules of the **elements** or **compounds** involved in the reaction must collide with each other. They must have enough energy to break the existing chemical bonds that join the molecules together and form new ones. The amount of energy needed for a chemical reaction to take place is known as the activation energy.

Hydrogen atom

Carbon atom

Methane molecule

Oxygen molecules

Oxygen atom

Carbon dioxide molecule

Methane and oxygen react to make carbon dioxide and water

Water molecules

In order for a chemical reaction to take place the molecules have to collide with each other with sufficient energy to break the bonds that hold them together.

Kinetics and gases

Chemical kinetics is especially important in the study of gases. All the explanations we have about the behaviour of gases come from kinetic theory, the idea of molecules in motion. Basically, all gases behave in a similar way at a specific **volume**, temperature and pressure. Kinetic theory says that all gases are composed of individual molecules in continuous random motion, colliding with each other and the walls of their container and so exerting pressure on it. The actual composition of the gas is not important in kinetic theory.

When the temperature is raised, the molecules of a gas gain energy and their speed increases. Because they are now hitting the walls of the container faster and more frequently, the pressure increases too. If more gas particles are added or if the volume of the container is reduced, the number of particles hitting the walls at any given time increases and so the pressure also increases.

Kinetic theory states that molecules are constantly moving in a random way.

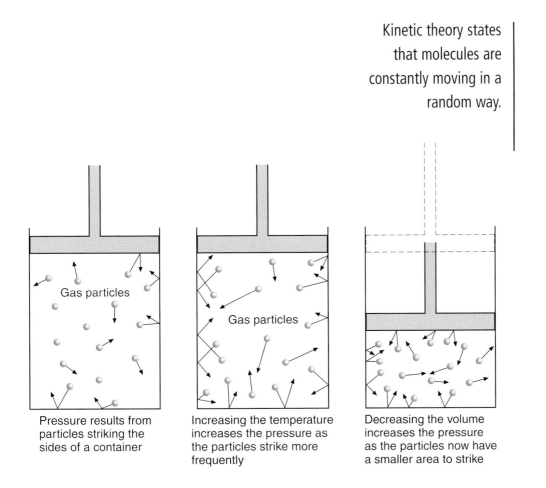

Pressure results from particles striking the sides of a container

Increasing the temperature increases the pressure as the particles strike more frequently

Decreasing the volume increases the pressure as the particles now have a smaller area to strike

The fourth state

In science classes only three states of matter are commonly described. We have met them all so far:
- solids, which have definite size and shape
- liquids, which have a definite volume and no definite shape
- gases, which have no definite size or shape.

What happens if we go on raising the temperature of a gas? If the temperature is raised to over 10,000°C, the **molecules** of the gas begin to collide with each other so violently that the **bonds** that hold them together are broken and they split into individual **atoms**. Negatively **charged electrons** are knocked off the atoms, which now have a positive charge. Charged atoms are called **ions**. Some atoms may remain completely intact and so a gas mixture, consisting of ions, electrons and neutral atoms, is produced. This mixture is called a plasma.

A plasma is a soup of atoms, electrons and ions.

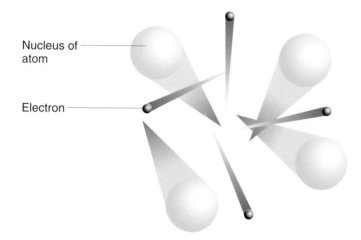

Nucleus of atom

Electron

Electric plasma

All these charged **particles** mean that a plasma is a good **conductor** of electricity. Apart from being very hot, a plasma differs from a gas because a plasma's movements are affected by electric and magnetic fields. In fact, the ions and the electrons in a plasma form an electric current, which in turn produces a magnetic field. The fact that a plasma can generate electric and magnetic fields, and is in turn affected by them, makes it behave in a way that is quite unlike any of the other three states of matter. The number of electrons and ions in the plasma are equal. So, although it has magnetic and electrical properties, overall a plasma is neutral.

Looking for plasmas

Plasmas exist in the hot centres of stars. The Sun is a 1.5-million-kilometre ball of plasma, heated by nuclear reactions at its core. The tails of comets are partly made of plasma from gases **ionized** by the energy of the Sun. Above the Earth's atmosphere, matter exists in the plasma state in the magnetosphere, the magnetic field that surrounds the Earth. Plasma in the magnetosphere is largely responsible for shielding Earth from cosmic **radiation**. Plasmas can also be found closer to home. Lightning can be thought of as a massive electrical discharge in the atmosphere that produces a plasma. When an electric current is passed through neon gas in a neon light, it produces light and plasma.

In a plasma atoms are stripped of electrons, forming a 'soup' of charged particles.

Plasma energy

*In an attempt to harness the **fusion** energy of stars here on Earth, physicists are studying devices that create and confine very hot plasmas in magnetic fields.*

Glossary

alloy mixture of two or more metals, or a metal and a non-metal

atom tiny particle from which all materials are made; the smallest part of an element that can exist

bonds forces that hold atoms together in molecules

brittle describes a substance that is hard but which will break or shatter easily

capillaries very thin tubes

charged having an electric charge

civil engineer an engineer who designs roads, bridges and similar structures

compound a substance that is made up of atoms of two or more elements

compressed flattened by pressure or squeezed into a smaller space

condensation point the temperature at which a gas becomes a liquid

condenser a piece of apparatus for condensing a gas, i.e. changing it to a liquid

conductor something that conducts heat or electricity

covalent a type of bond formed between atoms in which the atoms share electrons

crystals solids in which the atoms are arranged in a regular pattern

dense describes a substance in which the atoms or molecules from which it is made are packed closely together

electricity generators machines for generating electricity

electrons negatively-charged particles that are found in all atoms and that are the main carriers of electrical energy

element a substance that cannot be broken down into simpler substances by chemical reactions, an element is made up of just one type of atom

evaporate change into a vapour or a gas

evaporator a piece of apparatus in which evaporation takes place

fluid a substance that has no fixed shape; a gas or a liquid

friction force that acts to slow down or stop objects that are moving against each other

fusion when two small atoms combine to make a larger atom with the release of a great deal of energy

gravity force of attraction between objects

ion an atom or group of atoms that has an electric charge

ionic type of bond between atoms in which electrons are transferred from one atom to another

ionized describes an atom or molecule that has gained or lost electrons and so has an overall electric charge

kinetic energy energy of movement

latent heat heat taken in or given out when a substance changes from one state to another

lubricants substances that are used to reduce friction between moving parts of a machine

macromolecules molecules containing a very large number of atoms

mass the amount of matter that something contains

mechanical engineers engineers who design and construct machines

molecules two or more atoms combined together; if the atoms are the same it is an element, if they are different it is a compound

nuclear reactions reactions that involve changes to atoms

particles tiny portions of matter

piston a disc or cylinder that moves up and down inside a tube

pressure a force pushing on a given area

radiation high energy rays or particles; cosmic radiation comes from space

raw material material used in the manufacture of something

solvent a substance that can dissolve something

sublimation changing from a solid to a gas

surface tension a force in the surface of a liquid produced by the molecules at the surface being pulled by those below them

turbine a motor with a set of blades that rotate when pushed by a moving stream of liquid or gas

vaporise convert into a vapour or gas

vapour pressure the pressure produced by a liquid as it evaporates

volume the amount of space occupied by something

Index